THE VALIANT

A Play in One Act

BY

HOLWORTHY HALL

AND

ROBERT MIDDLEMASS

SAMUEL FRENCH LIMITED
LONDON

FOR AMATEUR PRODUCTION ENQUIRIES

UNITED KINGDOM AND WORLD
EXCLUDING NORTH AMERICA

plays@samuelfrench.co.uk

020 7255 4302/01

Each title is subject to availability from Samuel French, depending upon country of performance.

CHARACTERS

WARDEN HOLT (about 60).
FATHER DALY (the Prison Chaplain).
JAMES DYKE (the Prisoner).
JOSEPHINE PARIS (the Girl, about 18).
DAN (a Jailer).
AN ATTENDANT.

SCENE.—The Warden's office in the State Prison at Wethersfield, Connecticut.

TIME.—1921. About half-past eleven on a rainy night.

The fee for each and every representation of this play by amateurs is One Guinea, payable in advance to—

Messrs. Samuel French, Ltd.,
26 Southampton Street,
Strand, London, W.C.2,

or their authorized agents, who, upon payment of the fee, will issue a licence for the performance to take place.

No performance may be given unless this licence has been obtained.

The following particulars are needed for the issue of a licence:

Title of the play or plays.
Name of the town.
Name of the theatre or hall.
Date of the performance or performances.
Name and address of applicant.
Name of the Society.
Amount remitted.

Character costumes and wigs used in the performance of plays contained in French's Acting Edition may be obtained from Messrs. CHARLES H. FOX, Ltd., 184 High Holborn, London, W.C.1.

THE VALIANT

The Curtain *rises upon the* Warden's *office in the State Prison at Wethersfield, Connecticut. It is a large, cold, unfriendly apartment, with bare floors and staring, whitewashed walls; it is furnished only with the* Warden's *flat-topped desk and swivel-chair, with a few straight-backed chairs, one beside the desk and others against the walls, with an eight-day clock. On the* Warden's *desk are a telephone instrument, a row of electric bell-buttons, and a bundle of forty or fifty letters. At the back of the room are two large windows, crossed with heavy bars; at the* L. *there is a door to an anteroom, and at the* R. *there are two doors, of which the more distant leads to the office of the deputy warden, and the nearer is seldom used.*

Warden Holt, dressed in a dark brown suit, an open shirt and black string-tie, is seated at his desk, smoking a long, thin cigar. He is verging toward sixty, and his responsibilities have printed themselves in italics upon his countenance. His bearing indicates that he is accustomed to rank as a despot, and yet his expression is far from that of an unreasoning tyrant.

Behind the Warden, *the prison chaplain stands at one of the barred windows, gazing steadily out into the night.* Father Daly *is dressed in slightly shabby clericals. His face is calm, intellectual and inspiring; but just at this moment, it gives evidence of a peculiar depression.*

The Warden *blows a cloud of smoke to the ceiling, drums on the desk, and peers over his shoulder at the chaplain. He clears his throat and speaks brusquely.*

The Warden. Has it started to rain?

FATHER DALY (*answers without turning*).   Yes, it has.

THE WARDEN (*glaring at his cigar and impatiently tossing it aside*).   It *would* rain to-night.   (*His tone is vaguely resentful.*)

FATHER DALY (*glancing at a big silver watch*).   It's past eleven o'clock.   (*He draws a deep breath and comes slowly to the centre of the room.*)   We haven't much longer to wait.

THE WARDEN.   No, thank God!   Was he quiet when you left him?

FATHER DALY.   Yes, yes, he was perfectly calm, and I believe he'll stay so to the very end.

THE WARDEN (*lighting a fresh cigar*).   You've got to hand it to him, Father; I never saw such nerve in all my life.   It isn't bluff, and it isn't a trance, either, like some of 'em have—it's sheer nerve.   You've certainly got to hand it to him.   (*He shakes his head in frank admiration.*)

FATHER DALY.   That's the pity of it—that a man with all his courage hasn't a better use for it.   Even now, it's very difficult for me to reconcile his character, as I see it, with what we know he's done.

THE WARDEN (*continues to shake his head*).   He's got my goat, all right.

FATHER DALY (*with a slight grimace*).   Yes, and he's got mine, too.

THE WARDEN.   When he sent for you to-night, I hoped he was going to talk.

FATHER DALY.   He did talk, very freely.

THE WARDEN.   What about?

FATHER DALY (*smiles faintly, and sits beside the desk*). Almost everything.

THE WARDEN (*looks up quickly*).   Himself?

FATHER DALY.   No.   That seems to be the only subject he isn't interested in.

THE WARDEN (*sits up to his desk, and leans upon it with both elbows*).   He still won't give you any hint about who he really is?

FATHER DALY.   Not the slightest   He doesn't intend to, either.   He intends to die as a man of mystery to us. Sometimes I wonder if he isn't just as much of a mystery to himself.

THE WARDEN. Oh, he's trying to shield somebody, that's all. James Dyke isn't his real name—we know that; and we know all the rest of his story is a fake, too. Well, where's his motive? I'll tell you where it is. It's to keep his family and his friends, wherever they are, from knowing what's happened to him. Lots of 'em have the same idea, but I never knew one to carry it as far as this, before. You've certainly got to hand it to him. All we know is that we've got a man under sentence; and we don't know who he is, or where he comes from, or anything else about him, any more than we did four months ago.

FATHER DALY. It takes moral courage for a man to shut himself away from his family and his friends like that. They would have comforted him.

THE WARDEN. Not necessarily. What time is it?

FATHER DALY. Half-past eleven.

THE WARDEN (*rises and walks over to peer out of one of the barred windows*). I suppose I'm getting too old for this sort of thing. A hanging party didn't use to bother me so much; but every time one comes along nowadays, I've got the blue devils beforehand and afterwards. And this one is just about the limit.

FATHER DALY. It certainly isn't a pleasant duty even with the worst of them.

THE WARDEN (*wheels back abruptly*). But what riles *me* is why I should hate this one more than any of the others. The boy is guilty as hell.

FATHER DALY. Yes, he killed a man. " Wilfully, feloniously, and with malice aforethought."

THE WARDEN. And he pleaded guilty. So he deserves just what he's going to get.

FATHER DALY. That is the law. But has it ever occurred to you, Warden, that every now and then when a criminal behaves in a rather gentlemanly fashion to us, we instinctively think of him as just a little less of a criminal?

THE WARDEN. Yes, it has. But, all the same, this

front of his makes me as nervous as the devil. He pleaded guilty all right, but he doesn't *act* guilty. I feel just as if to-night I was going to do something every bit as criminal as he did. I can't help it. And when I start feeling like that, then I think it's about time I sent in my resignation.

FATHER DALY (*reflectively*). His whole attitude has been very remarkable. Why, only a few minutes ago I found myself comparing it with the fortitude that the Christian martyrs carried to their death, and yet——

THE WARDEN. He's no martyr.

FATHER DALY. I know. And he's anything in the world but a Christian. That was just what I was going to say.

THE WARDEN. Has he got any religious streak in him at all ?

FATHER DALY. I'm afraid he hasn't. He listens to me very attentively, but—— (*He shrugs his shoulders.*) It's only because I offer him companionship. Anybody else would do quite as well—and any other topic would suit him better.

THE WARDEN. Well, if he wants to face God as a heathen, *we* can't force him to change his mind.

FATHER DALY (*with gentle reproach*). No ; but we can never give up trying to save his immortal soul. And his soul to-night seems as dark and foreboding to me as a haunted house would seem to the small boys down in Wethersfield. But I haven't given up hope.

THE WARDEN. No—you wouldn't.

FATHER DALY. Are you going to talk to him again yourself ?

THE WARDEN (*opens a drawer of his desk, and brings out a large envelope*). I'll have to. I've still got some Liberty Bonds that belong to him. (*He gazes at the envelope, and smiles grimly.*) That was a funny thing—when the newspaper amalgamation offered him twenty-five hundred dollars for his autobiography, he jumped at it so quickly I was sure he wanted the money for something or other. (*He slaps the envelope on the desk.*) But now the bonds are here, waiting for him, he won't say what's to be done with 'em. Know why? (FATHER DALY *shakes his head.*) Why, of course you do! Because the story he wrote was pure bunk from start to finish and the only reason he jumped at the chance of writing it was so's he could pull the wool over everybody's head a little farther. He doesn't want the bonds, but I've got to do *something* with 'em. (*He pushes a button on the desk.*) And besides, I want to have one more try at finding out who he is.

FATHER DALY. Shall I go with you to see him or do you want to see him alone?

THE WARDEN (*sits deliberating with one hand at his forehead, and the other hand tapping the desk*). Father, you've given me a thought—I believe I'm going to do something to-night that's never been done before in this prison—that is to say—not in all the twenty-eight years that *I've* been warden.

FATHER DALY. What's that?

THE WARDEN (*who has come to an important decision, raps the desk more forcibly with his knuckles*). Instead of our going to see him, I'll have that boy brought into this office and let him sit here with you and me until the time comes for us all to walk through that door to the execution room.

FATHER DALY (*startled*). What on earth is your idea in doing a thing like that?

THE WARDEN. Because perhaps if he sits here with you and me, and we go at him in the right way, he'll tell us about himself. It'll be different from being in his cell; it'll be more free and easy, and maybe he'll weaken. And then, besides, if we take him to the scaffold through this passage-way, I can keep the others quiet. If they don't know when the job's being done, they may behave 'emselves. I don't want any such yelling and screeching to-night as we had over that Greek.

(*A* JAILER *in blue uniform enters from the deputy's room and stands waiting.*)

Dan, I want you to get Dyke and bring him to me here.

(*The* JAILER *stares blankly at him and the* WARDEN'S
  voice takes on an added note of authority.)

Get Dyke and bring him in here to me.
THE JAILER. Yes, sir.

(*He starts to obey the order but halts in the doorway and
  turns as the* WARDEN *speaks again. It is apparent
  that the* WARDEN *is a strict disciplinarian of the prison
  staff.*)

THE WARDEN. Oh, Dan !
THE JAILER. Yes, sir ?
THE WARDEN. How nearly ready are they ?
THE JAILER. They'll be finished in ten or fifteen
minutes, sir. Twenty minutes at the outside.
THE WARDEN (*very sharp and magisterial*). Now, I
don't want any hitch or delay in this thing to-night.
If there is, somebody's going to get in my bad books.
Pass that on.
THE JAILER. There won't be any, sir.
THE WARDEN. When everything's ready—not a
second before—you let me know.
THE JAILER. Yes, sir.
THE WARDEN. I'll be in here with Dyke and Father
Daly.
THE JAILER (*eyes widening*). Here ?
THE WARDEN (*peremptorily*). Yes, here !
THE JAILER (*crushes down his astonishment*). Yes, sir.
THE WARDEN. When everything and everybody is
ready, you come from the execution room through the
passage—(*he gestures toward the nearer door on the* R.)
—open that door quietly and stand there.
THE JAILER. Yes, sir.
THE WARDEN. You don't have to say anything, and
I don't *want* you to say anything. Just stand there.
That all clear ?
THE JAILER. Yes, sir.
THE WARDEN. That'll be the signal for us to start
—understand ?
THE JAILER. Yes, sir.

THE WARDEN (*draws a deep breath*). All right. Now bring Dyke to me.

THE JAILER. Yes, sir. (*He goes out dazedly.*)

FATHER DALY. What about the witnesses and the reporters?

THE WARDEN. They're having their sandwiches and coffee now—the deputy'll have 'em seated in another ten or fifteen minutes. Let 'em wait. (*His voice becomes savage.*) I'd like to poison the lot of 'em. Reporters! Witnesses! (*The telephone bell rings.*) Hello—yes—yes —what's that?—Yes, yes, here—who wants him? (*To* FATHER DALY.) Father, it's the Governor! (*His expression is tense.*)

FATHER DALY (*his voice also gives evidence of incredulity and hope*). What! (*He walks swiftly over to the desk.*) Is it about Dyke?

THE WARDEN. Ssh! (*He turns to the telephone.*) Yes, this is Warden Holt speaking. Hello—oh, hello, Governor Fuller, how are you? Oh, I'm hoary but healthy, thanks. Well, this isn't my idea of a picnic exactly—yes—yes—— Oh, I should say in about half an hour or so—everything's just about ready. (*His expression gradually relaxes, and* FATHER DALY, *with a little sigh and shake of the head, turns away.*) Oh, no, there won't be any slip—yes, we made the usual tests, one this afternoon and another at nine o'clock to-night—— Oh, no, Governor, nothing can go wrong—— Well, according to the law I've got to get it done as soon as possible after midnight, but you're the Governor of the state—— How long?—Certainly, Governor, I can hold it off as long as you want me to—— What's that?—A *girl*!—You're going to send her to me?—you *have* sent her!—she ought to be here by this time?—All right, Governor, I'll ring you up when it's over. Good-bye. (*He hangs up the receiver, mops his forehead with his handkerchief, and turns to* FATHER DALY *in great excitement.*) Did you hear *that*? Some girl thinks Dyke's her long-lost brother, and she's persuaded the old man to let her come out here to-night—he wants me to hold up the job until she's had a chance to see him. She's due here any minute, he says—in his own car—escorted by his own private secretary ! Can you beat it ?

FATHER DALY (*downcast*). Poor girl !

THE WARDEN (*blots his forehead vigorously*). For a minute there I thought it was going to be a reprieve at the very least. Whew !

FATHER DALY. So did I.

(*The door from the deputy's room is opened, and* DYKE *comes in, followed by the* JAILER. DYKE *halts just inside and waits passively to be told what to do next. He has a lean face, with a high forehead and a strong chin ; his mouth is a firm straight line. His hair is prematurely grey. His figure has the elasticity of youth, but he might pass among strangers either as a man of forty or as a man of twenty-five. He is dressed in a dark shirt open at the throat, dark trousers without belt or suspenders, and soft slippers. The* JAILER *receives a nod from the* WARDEN, *and goes out promptly, closing the door behind him.*)

THE WARDEN. Sit down, Dyke. (*He points to the chair at the* R. *of his desk.*)

DYKE. Thanks. (*He goes directly to the chair and sits down.*)

THE WARDEN (*leans back, and surveys him thoughtfully.* FATHER DALY *remains in the background*). Dyke, you've been here under my charge for nearly four months and I want to tell you that from first to last you've behaved yourself like a gentleman.

DYKE (*his manner is vaguely cynical without being in the least impertinent*). Why should I make any trouble ?

THE WARDEN. Well, you *haven't* made any trouble, and I've tried to show what I think about it. I've made you every bit as comfortable as the law would let me.

DYKE. You've been very kind to me. (*He glances over his shoulder at the chaplain.*) And you, too, Father.

THE WARDEN. I've had you brought in here to stay from now on. (DYKE *looks inquiringly at him.*) No, you won't have to go back to your cell again. You're to stay here with Father Daly and me.

DYKE (*carelessly*). All right.

THE WARDEN (*piqued by this cool reception of the distinguished favour*). You don't seem to understand that I'm doing something a long way out of the ordinary for you.

DYKE. Oh, yes, I do; but it's possible *you* don't understand why it doesn't give me much of a thrill.

FATHER DALY (*comes forward*). My son, the Warden is only trying to do you one more kindness.

DYKE. I know he is, Father; but the Warden isn't taking very much of a gamble. From now on, one place is about the same as another.

THE WARDEN. What do you mean?

DYKE (*his voice is very faintly sarcastic*). I mean that I'm just as much a condemned prisoner here as when I was in my cell. That door (*he points to it*) leads straight *back* to my cell. Outside those windows are armed guards every few feet. You yourself can't get through the iron door in that anteroom (*he indicates the door to the* L.) until somebody on the outside unlocks it; and I know as well as you do where *that* door (*he points to the nearer door on the* R.) leads to.

THE WARDEN (*stiffly*). Would you rather wait in your cell?

DYKE. Oh, no, this is a little pleasanter. Except——

THE WARDEN. Except what?

DYKE. I could smoke in my cell.

THE WARDEN (*shrugs his shoulders*). What do you want—cigar or cigarette?

DYKE. A cigarette, if it's all the same.

(*The* WARDEN *opens a drawer of his desk, takes out a box of cigarettes, removes one and hands it to* DYKE. *The* WARDEN *striking a match, lights* DYKE'S *cigarette, and then carefully puts out the match.*)

DYKE (*smiles faintly*). Thanks. You're a good host.

THE WARDEN. Dyke, before it's too late, I wish you'd think over what Father Daly and I've said to you so many times.

DYKE. I've thought of nothing else.

THE WARDEN. Then—as man to man—and this is your last chance—who are you?

DYKE (*inspects his cigarette*). Who am I? James Dyke—a murderer.

THE WARDEN. That isn't your real name and we know it.

DYKE. You're not going to execute a name—you're going to execute a *man*. What difference does it make whether you call me Dyke or something else?

THE WARDEN. You had another name once. What was it?

DYKE. If I had, I've forgotten it.

FATHER DALY. Your mind is made up, my son?

DYKE. Yes, Father, it is.

THE WARDEN. Dyke.

DYKE. Yes, sir?

THE WARDEN. Do you see this pile of letters? (*He places his hand over it.*)

DYKE. Yes, sir.

THE WARDEN (*fingers them*). Every one of these letters is about the same thing and all put together we've got about four thousand of 'em. These are just a few samples.

DYKE. What about them?

THE WARDEN. We've had letters from every State in the Union and every province in Canada. We've had fifteen or twenty from England, four or five from France, two from Australia and one from Russia.

DYKE. Well?

THE WARDEN. Do you know what every one of those letters says—what four thousand different people are writing to me about?

DYKE. No, sir.

THE WARDEN (*speaks slowly and impressively*). Who *are* you—and are you the missing son—or brother—or husband—or sweetheart?

DYKE (*flicks his cigarette ashes to the floor*). Have you answered them?

THE WARDEN. No, I couldn't. I want you to.

DYKE. How's that?

THE WARDEN. I want you to tell me who you are. (DYKE *shakes his head*.) Can't you see you *ought* to do it ?

DYKE. No, sir, I can't see that exactly. Suppose you explain it to me.

THE WARDEN (*suddenly*). You're trying to shield somebody, aren't you ?

DYKE. Yes—no, I'm not !

THE WARDEN (*glances at* FATHER DALY *and nods with elation*). Who is it ? Your family ?

DYKE. I said I'm not.

THE WARDEN. But first, you said you were.

DYKE. That was a slip of the tongue.

THE WARDEN (*has grown persuasive*). Dyke, just listen to me a minute. Don't be narrow, look at this in a big, broad way. Suppose you should tell me your real name, and I publish it, it'll bring an awful lot of sorrow, let's say, to *one* family, *one* home, and that's your own. That's probably what you're thinking about. Am I right ? You want to spare your family and I don't blame you. On the surface, it would look like a fine, white thing for you to do. But look at it *this* way : suppose you came out with the stark truth, why, then you might put all that sorrow into *one* home—your own —but at the same time you'd be putting an immense amount of relief in four thousand—others. Don't you see that ? Don't you feel you owe something to all these other people ?

DYKE. Not a thing.

FATHER DALY (*has been fidgeting*). My boy, the Warden is absolutely right. You do owe something to the other people—you owe them peace of mind—and for the sake of all those thousands of poor, distressed women, who imagine God knows what, I beg of you to tell us who you are.

DYKE. Father, I simply can't do it.

FATHER DALY. Think carefully, my boy, think very carefully. We're not asking out of idle curiosity.

DYKE. I know that ; but please don't let's talk about it any more. You can answer those letters whenever you

want to, and you can say I'm not the man they're looking
for. That'll be the truth, anyway. Because I haven't
any mother—or father—or sister—or wife—or sweetheart. That's fair enough, isn't it?

FATHER DALY. As you will, my son.

THE WARDEN. Dyke, there's one thing more.

DYKE. Yes?

THE WARDEN. Here are the Liberty Bonds (*he takes
up the large envelope from his desk*) that belong to you.
Twenty-five hundred dollars in real money.

DYKE (*removes the bonds and examines them*). Good-
looking, aren't they?

THE WARDEN (*casually*). What do you want me to
do with them?

DYKE. Well, I can't very well take them with me, so,
under the circumstances, I'd like to put them where
they'll do the most good.

THE WARDEN (*more casually yet*). Who do you want
me to send 'em to?

DYKE (*laughs quietly*). Now, Warden Holt, you didn't
think you were going to catch me that way, did you?

THE WARDEN (*scowls*). Who'll I send 'em to? I
can't keep 'em here, and I can't destroy 'em. What do
you want to do with 'em?

DYKE (*ponders diligently and tosses the envelopes to the
desk*). I don't know. I'll think of something to do with
them. I'll tell you in just a minute. Is there anything
else?

THE WARDEN. Not unless you want to make some
sort of statement.

DYKE. No, I think I've said everything. I killed a
man and I'm not sorry for it—that is, I'm not sorry I
killed that particular person. I——

FATHER DALY (*raises his hand*). Repentance——

DYKE (*raises his own hand in turn*). I've heard that
repentance, Father, is the sick-bed of the soul—and mine
is very well and flourishing. The man deserved to be
killed; he wasn't fit to live. It was my duty to kill
him, and I did it. I'd never struck a man in anger in all
my life, but when I knew what that fellow had done, I

knew I had to kill him, and I did it deliberately and intentionally—and carefully. I knew what I was doing, and I haven't any excuse—that is, I haven't any excuse that satisfies the law. Now, I learned pretty early in life that whatever you do in this world you have to pay for in one way or another. If you kill a man, the price you have to pay is this (*he makes a gesture which sweeps the entire room*) and that (*he points to the nearer door on the* R.) and I'm going to pay it. That's all there is to that. And an hour from now, while my body is lying in there, if a couple of angel policemen grab my soul and haul it up before God——

FATHER DALY (*profoundly shocked*). My boy, my boy, please——

DYKE. I beg your pardon, Father. I don't mean to trample on anything that's sacred to you; but what I do mean to say is this: If I've got to be judged by God Almighty for the crime of murder, I'm not afraid, because the other fellow will certainly be there, too, won't he? And when God hears the whole story and both sides of it, which *you* never heard and never will—and they never heard it in the court room, either—well, then, if he's any kind of a God at all, I'm willing to take my chances with the other fellow. That's how concerned I am about the hereafter. And, if it'll make you feel any better, Father, I *do* rather think there's going to be a hereafter. I read a book once that said a milligramme of musk will give out perfume for seven thousand years, and a milligramme of radium will give out light for *seventy* thousand. Why shouldn't a soul—mine, for instance—live more than twenty-seven? But if there *isn't* any hereafter—if we just die and are dead and that's all—I'm still not sorry and I'm not afraid, because I'm quits with the other fellow—the law is quits with me, and it's all balanced on the books. And that's all there is to be said.

(*An* ATTENDANT *enters from the anteroom.*)

THE WARDEN. Well? What is it?

THE ATTENDANT. Visitor to see you, sir. With a note from Governor Fuller. (*He presents it.*)

THE WARDEN (*barely glances at the envelope*). Oh ! A young woman ?

THE ATTENDANT. Yes, sir.

THE WARDEN. Is Mrs. Case there ?

THE ATTENDANT. Yes, sir.

THE WARDEN. Have the girl searched, and then take her into the anteroom and wait till I call you.

THE ATTENDANT. Yes, sir. (*He goes out.*)

THE WARDEN. Dyke, a young woman has just come to see you—do you want to see her ?

DYKE. I don't think so. What does she want ?

THE WARDEN. She thinks perhaps she's your sister, and she's come a thousand miles to find out.

DYKE. She's wrong. I haven't any sister.

THE WARDEN (*hesitates*). Shall I tell her that, or do you want to tell her yourself ?

DYKE. Oh, you tell her.

THE WARDEN. All right.

DYKE. Just a second—she's come a thousand miles to see me, did you say ?

THE WARDEN. Yes, and she's got special permission from the Governor to talk to you—that is, with my O.K.

DYKE. A year ago, nobody'd have crossed the street to look at me, and now they come a thousand miles !

FATHER DALY. This is one of your debts to humanity, my boy. It wouldn't take you two minutes to see her, and, if you don't, after she's made that long journey in hope and dread and suffering——

DYKE. Where can I talk to her—here ?

THE WARDEN. Yes.

DYKE. Alone ? You needn't be afraid. I haven't the faintest idea who the girl is ; but if she happens to be some poor misguided sentimental fool, with a gun or a pocket full of cyanide of potassium, she's wasting her time. I wouldn't cheat the sovereign state of Connecticut for anything in the world—not even to please a young lady.

THE WARDEN. Dyke, there's something about you that wins everybody.

DYKE. How about the jury ?

THE WARDEN. You've got a way with you——

DYKE. What about that swollen-headed district attorney ?

THE WARDEN. I'm going to let you talk to that girl in here—alone.

DYKE. Thanks.

THE WARDEN. It's a sort of thing that's never been done before, but if I put you on your honour——

DYKE (*cynically*). My honour ! Thank you, so much.

FATHER DALY. Warden, are you sure it's wise ?

DYKE. Father, I'm disappointed in you. Do you imagine I'd do anything that could reflect on Warden Holt—or you—or the young lady—or *me* ?

THE WARDEN. Father, will you take Dyke into the deputy's room ? I want to speak to the young lady first.

FATHER DALY. Certainly. Come, my boy.

THE WARDEN. I'll call you in two minutes.

DYKE. We promise not to run away.

(*They go out together.*)

THE WARDEN (*calls*). Wilson !

(*The* ATTENDANT *enters from the* L.)

THE ATTENDANT. Yes, sir.

THE WARDEN. Is the girl there ?

THE ATTENDANT. Yes, sir.

THE WARDEN. Been searched ?

THE ATTENDANT. Yes, sir.

THE WARDEN. Everything all right ?

THE ATTENDANT. Yes, sir.

THE WARDEN (*throws away his cigar*). Bring her in.

THE ATTENDANT. Yes, sir. (*He speaks through the door at the* L.) Step this way, miss. This is the Warden.

(*A young* GIRL *appears ; she is fresh and wholesome, and rather pretty ; but her manner betrays a certain spiritual aloofness from the ultra-modern world which separates her from the metropolitan class. She is dressed simply and wears a blue tailored suit with deep white cuffs and a starched white sailor-collar, and a small blue hat over her fluffy hair. Her costume hints at the taste and repression of an old-fashioned home.*

She is neither timid nor aggressive; she is self-unconscious. Her expression is essentially serious due to her present mission; ordinarily she takes an active joy in the mere pleasure of existence.)

THE WARDEN (*he had expected a very different type of visitor*). All right, Wilson.

THE ATTENDANT. Yes, sir. (*He goes out.*)

THE WARDEN (*with grave deference, half rises*). Will you sit down?

THE GIRL. Thank you very much. (*She sits and regards him trustfully.*)

THE WARDEN (*affected by her youth and innocence, he is not quite sure how to proceed*). You've had an interview with the Governor, I understand?

THE GIRL. Yes, sir. I was with him almost an hour.

THE WARDEN. And you want to see Dyke, do you?

THE GIRL. Yes, sir. I *hope* I'm not—too late.

THE WARDEN. No, you're not too late. But I want to ask you a few questions beforehand. (*Her reaction of uncertainty induces him to soften his tone.*) There isn't anything to get upset about. I just want to make it easier for you, not harder. Where do you live?

THE GIRL. In Ohio.

THE WARDEN. What place?

THE GIRL. In Pennington, sir. It's a little town not far from Columbus.

THE WARDEN. And you live out there with your father and mother?

THE GIRL. No, sir—just my mother and I. My father died when I was a little baby.

THE WARDEN. Why didn't your mother come here herself, instead of sending you?

THE GIRL. She couldn't. She's ill.

THE WARDEN. I see. Have you any brothers or sisters?

THE GIRL. Just one brother, sir—this one. He and I

were the only children. We were very fond of each other.

THE WARDEN. He was considerably older than you?

THE GIRL. Oh, yes. He's ten years older.

THE WARDEN. Why did he leave home?

THE GIRL. I don't really know, sir, except that he wanted to be in the city. Pennington's rather small.

THE WARDEN. How long is it since you've seen him?

THE GIRL. It's eight years.

THE WARDEN (*his voice is almost paternal*). As long as that? Hm! And how old are you now?

THE GIRL. I'm almost eighteen.

THE WARDEN. Almost eighteen. Hm! And are you sure after all this time you'd recognize your brother if you saw him?

THE GIRL. Well—of course I *think* so; but perhaps I couldn't. You see, I was only a little girl when he went away—he wasn't a bad boy, sir, I don't think he could ever be really bad—but if this *is* my brother, then he's been in a great deal of trouble and you know that trouble makes people look different.

THE WARDEN. Yes, it does. But what makes you think this man Dyke may be your brother—and why didn't you think of it sooner? The case has been in the papers for the last six months.

THE GIRL. Why, it wasn't until last Tuesday that mother saw something in the " Journal "—that's the Columbus paper—that he'd written all about himself, and there was one little part of it that sounded so like Joe —like the funny way he used to say things—and then there was a picture that looked the least little *bit* like him—well, mother just wanted me to come East and find out for certain.

THE WARDEN. It's too bad she couldn't come herself. She'd probably know him whether he'd changed or not.

THE GIRL. Yes, sir. But I'll do the best I can.

THE WARDEN. When was the last time you heard from him, and where was he, and what was he doing?

THE GIRL. It's about five or six years since we had a letter from Joe. He was in Seattle, Washington.

THE WARDEN. What was he doing?

THE GIRL. I don't remember. At home, though, he worked in the stationery shop. He liked books.

THE WARDEN (*suspiciously*). Why do you suppose he didn't write home?

THE GIRL. I—couldn't say. He was just—thoughtless.

THE WARDEN. He wasn't in trouble of any kind?

THE GIRL. Oh, *no*! Never. That is—unless he's—here now.

THE WARDEN (*deliberates*). How are you going to tell him?

THE GIRL. I don't know what you mean.

THE WARDEN. Why, you say perhaps you wouldn't know him even if you saw him—and I'll guarantee this man Dyke won't help you out very much. How do you think you're going to tell? Suppose he doesn't want to be recognized by you or anybody else? Suppose he's so ashamed of himself he——

THE GIRL. I'd thought of that. I'm just going to talk to him—ask him questions—about things he and I used to do together—I'll watch his face, and if he's my brother, I'm sure I can tell.

THE WARDEN. What did you and your brother ever use to do that would help you now?

THE GIRL. He used to play games with me when I was a little girl, and tell me stories—that's what I'm counting on most of all—the stories.

THE WARDEN. I'm afraid——

THE GIRL. Especially Shakespeare stories.

THE WARDEN. Shakespeare!

THE GIRL. Why, yes. He used to get the plots of the plays—all the Shakespeare plays—out of a book by a man named Lamb, and then he'd tell me the stories in his own words. It was wonderful!

THE WARDEN. I'm certainly afraid he——

THE GIRL. But best of all he'd learn some of the speeches from the plays themselves. He liked to do it —he was sure he was going to be an actor or something —he was in all the high school plays, always. And then he'd teach me some of the speeches, and we'd say them to each other. And one thing—every night he'd sit beside my bed, and when I got sleepy there were two speeches we'd always say to each other, as a good-night—two speeches out of *Romeo and Juliet*, and then I'd go to sleep. I can see it all. (*The* WARDEN *shakes his head.*) Why do you do that?

THE WARDEN. This boy isn't your brother.

THE GIRL. Do you think he isn't?

THE WARDEN. I *know* he isn't.

THE GIRL. How do you?

THE WARDEN. This boy never heard of Shakespeare —much less learned him. (*He presses a button on his desk.*) Oh, I'll let you see him for yourself, only you might as well be prepared.

(*The* ATTENDANT *enters from the anteroom.*)

Tell Dyke and Father Daly to come in here—they're in the deputy's room.

THE ATTENDANT. Yes, sir. (*He goes off.*)

THE WARDEN. If he turns out to be your brother— which he won't—you can have, say, an hour with him. If he does not, you'll oblige me by cutting it as short as you can.

THE GIRL. You see, I've got to tell mother something perfectly definite. She's worried so long about him, and —and *now* the suspense is perfectly terrible for her.

THE WARDEN. I can understand that. You're a plucky girl.

THE GIRL. Of course, it would be awful for us if this *is* Joe, but even that would be better for mother than just to stay awake at nights, and wonder and wonder, and never *know* what has become of him.

(*The* ATTENDANT *opens the door of the Deputy's room, and when* DYKE *and* FATHER DALY *have come in, he is going out when the* WARDEN *signs to him and he stops.*)

THE WARDEN. Dyke, this is the young lady that's come all the way from Pennington, Ohio, to see you.

DYKE (*who has been talking in an undertone to* FATHER DALY, *raises his head quickly*). Yes, sir?

THE WARDEN. I've decided you can talk with her here—alone.

(*The* GIRL *has risen, breathless, and stands fixed;* DYKE *inspects her coldly from head to foot.*)

DYKE. Thank you. It won't take long.

THE WARDEN (*has been scanning the* GIRL'S *expression; now, as he sees that she has neither recognized* DYKE *nor failed to recognize him, he makes a little grimace in confirmation of his own judgment*). Father Daly and I'll stay in the deputy's office. We'll leave the door open. Wilson, you stand in the anteroom with the door open.

DYKE (*bitterly*). My honour!

THE WARDEN. What do you say?

DYKE. I didn't say anything.

THE WARDEN. Will you please remember what I told you about the time?

THE GIRL. Oh, yes, sir.

THE WARDEN. Come, Father.

(*They go off into the* Deputy's *room, and the* ATTENDANT *goes off at the* L.)

(DYKE *and the* GIRL *are now facing each other;* DYKE *gives the impression of complete indifference to the moment. The* GIRL *is deeply agitated.*)

THE GIRL (*after several efforts to speak*). Mother sent me to see you.

DYKE (*politely callous*). Yes?

THE GIRL. You see, we haven't seen or heard of my brother Joe for ever so long, and Mother thought—after what we read in the papers——

DYKE. That I might be your brother Joe?

THE GIRL. Yes, that's it.

DYKE. Well, you can easily see that I'm not your brother, can't you?

THE GIRL (*stares at him again*). I'm not sure. You look a little like him, just as the picture in the paper did, but then again, it's so long—and I'd thought of Joe so differently——

Dyke (*his manner is somewhat indulgent, as though to a child*). As a matter of fact, I couldn't be *your* brother, or anybody else's brother, because I never had a sister. So that rather settles it.

The Girl. Honestly ?

Dyke. Honestly.

The Girl (*unconvinced*). What's your real name ?

Dyke. Dyke—James Dyke.

The Girl. That's really your name ?

Dyke. Really. You don't think I'd tell a lie at this stage of the game, do you ?

The Girl. No, I don't believe you would. Where do you come from—I mean where were you born ?

Dyke. In Canada, but I've lived everywhere.

The Girl. Didn't you ever live in Ohio ?

Dyke. No. Never.

The Girl. What kind of work did you do—what was your business ?

Dyke. Oh, I'm sort of Jack-of-all-trades. I've been everything a man *could* be—except a success.

The Girl. Do you like books ?

Dyke. Books ?

The Girl. Yes—books to read.

Dyke. I don't read when there's anything better to do. I've read a lot here.

The Girl. Did you ever sell books—for a living, I mean ?

Dyke. Oh, no.

The Girl (*growing confused*). I hope you don't mind my asking so many questions. But I——

Dyke. No—go ahead, if it'll relieve your mind at all.

The Girl. You went to school somewhere, of course—high school ?

Dyke. No, I never got that far.

The Girl. Did you ever want to be an actor ? Or *were* you ever ?

Dyke. No, just a convict.

The Girl (*helplessly*). Do you know any poetry ?

Dyke. Not to speak of.

THE GIRL (*watching him very earnestly, she recites just above her breath*). " Thou know'st the mask of night is on my face,

Else would a maiden blush bepaint my cheek
For that which——"

(DYKE'S *expression is one of utter vacuity ; she breaks off the quotation, but continues to watch him unwaveringly.*)

Don't you know what that is ?

DYKE. No, but to tell the truth, it sounds rather silly to *me*. Doesn't it to you ?

THE GIRL (*her intonation has become slightly forlorn, but she gathers courage*). " Good-night, good-night ! parting is such sweet sorrow

That I shall say good-night till it be morrow."

DYKE. Eh ?

THE GIRL. What comes next ?

DYKE. Good Lord, *I* don't know.

THE GIRL (*gazes intently at him as though she is making a struggle to read his mind. Then she relaxes and holds out her hand*). Good-bye. You—you're *not* Joe, are you ? I—had to come and find out, though. I hope I've not made you too unhappy.

DYKE. You're not going now ?

THE GIRL (*spiritless*). Yes. I promised the—is he the Warden ? that man in there ?—I said I'd go away at once if you weren't my brother. And you aren't, so——

DYKE. You're going back to your mother ?

THE GIRL. Yes.

DYKE. I'm surprised that she sent a girl like you on a sorry errand like this, instead of——

THE GIRL. She's very ill.

DYKE. Oh, that's too bad.

THE GIRL. No, she's not well at all. And most of it's from worrying about Joe.

DYKE. Still, when you tell her that her son isn't a murderer—at least, that he isn't *this* one—that'll comfort her a good deal, won't it ?

THE GIRL. Yes, I think maybe it will; only——

DYKE. Only what?

THE GIRL. I don't think mother'll ever be *really* well again until she finds out for certain where Joe is and what's become of him.

DYKE (*shakes his head compassionately*). Mothers ought not to be treated like that. I wish I'd treated *mine* better. By the way, you didn't tell me what your name is.

THE GIRL. Josephine Paris.

DYKE (*is suddenly attentive*). Paris? That's an unusual name. I've heard it somewhere, too.

THE GIRL. Just like the name of the city—in France.

DYKE. And your brother's name was Joseph?

THE GIRL. Yes—they used to call us Joe and Josie—that's funny, isn't it?

DYKE (*thoughtfully*). No, I don't think it's so very funny. I rather like it. (*He passes his hand over his forehead as if trying to coerce his memory.*)

THE GIRL. What's the matter?

DYKE (*frowning*). I was thinking of something—now, what on earth was that boy's name! Wait a minute, don't tell me—wait a minute—I've got it! (*He punctuates his triumph with one fist in the palm of the other hand.*) Joseph Anthony Paris!

THE GIRL (*amazed*). Why, that's his name! That's Joe! How did you ever——

DYKE (*his manner is very forcible and convincing*). Wait! Now listen carefully to what I say, and don't interrupt me, because we've only got a minute, and I want you to get this all clear, so that you can tell your mother. When the war came I enlisted and I was overseas for four years—with the Canadians. Early one morning we'd staged a big trench raid, and there was an officer who'd been wounded coming back, who was lying out there in a shell-hole under fire. The Jerries were getting ready for a raid of their own, so they were putting down a box barrage with light guns and howitzers and a few heavies. This officer was lying right in the middle of it. Well, all of a sudden a young fellow dashed out of a trench not far from where I was, and went for that officer. He had to go through a curtain of shells and, more than that, they opened on him with rifles and machine guns. The chances were just about a million to one against him, and he must have known it, but he went out just the same. He got the officer in his arms and started back, but he'd only gone a few yards when a five-point-nine landed right on top of the two of them. Afterward, we got what was left—the identification tag was still there—and that was the name—Joseph Anthony Paris!

THE GIRL (*carries both hands to her breast*). Oh!

DYKE. If that was your brother's name, then you can tell your mother that he died like a brave man and a soldier, three years ago, in France.

THE GIRL. Joe—my brother Joe—is dead?

DYKE. On the field of battle. It was one of the wonderful, heroic things that went almost unnoticed, as so many of them did. If an officer had seen it, there'd have been a decoration for your mother to keep and remember him by.

THE GIRL. And you were there—and saw it?

DYKE. I was there and saw it. It was three years ago. That's why you and your mother haven't heard from him. And if you don't believe what I've said, you can write up to Ottawa and get the official record. Of course those records are in terribly poor shape, but at least they can tell you what battalion he fought with, when he went overseas. Only you mustn't be surprised no matter whether they say he was killed in action, or died of wounds, or is missing, or even went through the whole war with his outfit, and was honourably discharged. They really don't know what happened to half the men. But I've told you the truth. And it certainly ought to make your mother happy when she knows that her boy died as a soldier, and not as a criminal.

THE GIRL. Yes, yes, it will!

DYKE. And does it make you happy, too?

THE GIRL (*nods repeatedly*). Yes. So happy—after what we were both afraid of—I can't even cry—yet. I can hardly wait to take it to her.

DYKE (*struck by a sudden inspiration*). I want to give you something else to take to her. (*He picks up from the desk the envelope containing the Liberty Bonds and seals it.*) I want you to give this to your mother from me. Tell her it's from a man who was at Vimy Ridge and saw your brother die, so it's a sort of memorial for him. (*He touches her arm as she absently begins to tear open the envelope.*) No, don't you open it—let *her* do it.

THE GIRL. What is it? Can't I know?

DYKE. Never mind now, but give it to her. It's all I've got in the world and it's too late now for me to do anything else with it. And now I'm afraid it *is* time for you to go. I'm sorry, but—you'd better. I'm glad you came before it was too late, though.

THE GIRL (*gives him her hand*). Good-bye, and thank you. You've done more for me—and mother—than I could possibly tell you. And—and I'm so sorry for you—so *truly sorry*—I wish I could only do something to make you a tiny bit happier, too. Is there anything I could do?

DYKE (*stares at her and by degrees he becomes wistful*). Why—yes, there is. Only I——

THE GIRL. What is it?

DYKE (*looks away*). I can't tell you. I never should have let myself think of it.

THE GIRL. Please tell me. I want you to. For—for Joe's sake, tell me what I can do.

DYKE (*his voice is low and desolate*). Well—in all the months I've been in this hideous place, you're the first girl I've seen. I didn't ever expect to see one again. I'd forgotten how much like angels women look. I've been terribly lonely to-night, especially, and if you really do want to do something for me—for your brother's sake—you see, you're going to leave me in just a minute and—and I haven't any sister of my own, or anybody else, to say good-bye to me—so, if you could—*really* say good-bye—— (*She gazes at him for a moment, understands, flushes, and then slowly moves into his outstretched arms. He holds her close to him, touches his lips to her forehead twice, and releases her.*)

DYKE (*thickly*). Good-bye, my dear.

THE GIRL. Good night. (*She endeavours to smile, but her voice catches in her throat.*) Good-bye.

DYKE (*impulsively*). What is it?

THE GIRL (*shakes her head*). N-nothing.

DYKE. Nothing?

THE GIRL. I was thinking—I was thinking what I used to say to my brother—as good night. (*She very nearly breaks down.*) If *only* I could have—have said it to him just once more—as good-bye.

DYKE. What was it?

THE GIRL. I—I told it to you once, and you said it was silly.

DYKE (*softly*). Say it again.

THE GIRL (*she cannot quite control her voice*). " Good-night, good-night! parting is such sweet sorrow That I shall say good-night till it be morrow."

(*She goes toward the anteroom, hesitates, and then with a choking sob she hurries through the door and closes it behind her. For several seconds DYKE stands rigidly intent upon that door; until at length, without changing his attitude or his expression, he speaks very tenderly and reminiscently.*)

" Sleep dwell upon thine eyes, peace in thy breast! Would I were sleep and peace, so sweet to rest!"

(*The WARDEN and FATHER DALY come in quietly from the Deputy's room; and as they behold DYKE, rapt and unconscious of them, they look at each other, questioningly. The Chaplain sits down in one of the chairs at the back wall; the WARDEN crosses on tiptoe and sits at his desk; he is excessively nervous and he continually refers to the clock. DYKE turns from the door; his thoughts are evidently far away. He sits in the chair to the R. of the WARDEN'S desk and leans outward, his right hand on his knee. He puts his left hand to his throat as though to protect it from a sudden pain. He gazes straight ahead into the unknown and speaks in reverie.*)

" Of all the wonders that I yet have heard,
It seems to me most strange that men should fear ;
Seeing that death, a necessary end,
Will come when it will come."

(*He stops and muses for a time, while the* WARDEN *glances perplexedly at* FATHER DALY ; *the priest shakes his head.* DYKE'S *face is illumined by a new and welcome recollection ; and again he speaks, while the* WARDEN *tries in vain to comprehend him.*)

" Cowards die many times before their deaths ;
The valiant never taste of death but once."

(*He stops again and shudders a trifle ; his head droops and he repeats, barely above a whisper.*)

" The valiant never taste of death but once."

{*The nearer door on the* R. *is opened and the* JAILER *steps just inside the room and stands mute.* FATHER DALY *and the* WARDEN *glance at the* JAILER, *and with signifi· cance at each other, and both rise, tardily. The* WAR- DEN'S *hand, as it rests on his desk, is seen to tremble. There is a moment of dead silence ; presently* DYKE *lifts his head and catches sight of the motionless* ATTEND- ANT *at the open door. He turns his head to gaze first at* FATHER DALY *and then at the* WARDEN. *The* WARDEN *averts his eyes, but* FATHER DALY'S *expression is of supreme pity and encouragement. Involuntarily,* DYKE'S *hand again goes creeping upward toward his throat, but he arrests it. He braces himself ; he rises and stands very erect, in almost the position of a soldier at attention.*)

THE WARDEN. Dyke !
FATHER DALY (*his right hand lifted as though in bene- diction*). My son !
DYKE (*regards them fixedly ; his voice is low and steady*). All right, let's go.

(*He faces about, and with his head held proud and high, and his shoulders squared, he moves slowly toward the open door. FATHER DALY steps in line just ahead of DYKE. The WARDEN, his mouth set hard, falls in behind. When they have all gone forward a pace or two, FATHER DALY begins to speak, and DYKE to reply; FATHER DALY's voice is strong and sweet; DYKE speaks just after him in brave and unfaltering response.)*

FATHER DALY. "I will lift up mine eyes unto the hills——"

DYKE. "The valiant never taste of death but once."

FATHER DALY. "From whence cometh my help."

DYKE. "The valiant never taste of death but once."

FATHER DALY (*has almost reached the door; his voice rises a semitone, and gains in emotion*). "My help cometh from the Lord which made Heaven and earth."

DYKE. "The valiant never taste of death—but once."

(When the WARDEN has passed the threshold, the JAILER follows and closes the door behind him. There is a very brief pause and

The CURTAIN *falls.*